THOSE WHO

SHOUT LOUDEST

THOSE WHO SHOUT LOUDEST

"I love to work. If I'm awake I'm working. But work isn't working for me, working for me is the way I am, it's just fun."

Tom Ford

THOSE WHO SHOUT LOUDEST

So, let's begin.

They say money runs the world, but really it's marketing.

Advertising dictates where money is spent, which public figures we follow, and decides what news stories generate media companies the most revenue (due to advertising revenue being one of the primary ways that news platforms monetise their articles).

Many see this as a scary change in society that is leading us down a road towards dystopia. In actuality, advertising tools are now more accessible than ever, and anyone can utilise them to promote their brand (personal or business).

A small bakery can now stand toe-to-toe with Greggs in its city, reaching thousands of hungry homes within its local area using a small advertising budget.

In the past, this wasn't possible. TV, radio, and news paper ads were generally dominated by big brands, and small businesses simply didn't have the money to pay for them. If they did, they'd be paying for the worst ad spots, generally proving ineffective of actually reaching their desired audience.

THOSE WHO SHOUT LOUDEST

Nowadays, the advertising tools available for brands is incredible. From simply paying to reach as many people as possible on social media, to creating an interactive storytelling experience through your website; there are enough options to fit anyone's vision.

This doesn't just refer to businesses either.

If you create videos, make music, write articles, do photography, are part of a group with a common interest, or anything else you can really think of; advertising has granted you considerably more opportunities for growth than you could possibly realise.

That's not to say everything about advertising is inherently good, it's not. In the words of Uncle Ben (from Spider-man), "with great power comes great responsibility", and he's right.

Of course this does refer to those annoying ads we constantly see before watching a video on YouTube, but it also refers to how these ads can be used to influence our emotions and distort opinions.

It's generally accepted by all sides of the political spectrum that the 2016 U.S election and Brexit was dictated by an extremely aggressive marketing strategy, rather than the political parties' policies.

THOSE WHO SHOUT LOUDEST

Advertising was used to divide the nations, forcing individuals into one of two categories: right or left. In real life, everyone's political values are extremely unique. The likelihood of one political party aligning with all of your core ethical values is absurd, but during these elections we've seen huge amounts of the population become territorial about their chosen political party.

It becomes a case of "if you don't vote for *insert political party here*, you're a *insert name-calling here*".

The issue isn't that one or two political parties exercise this approach either, it's that all of them do.

Polarising individuals and gaslighting them into aligning with one political party is now part of every election cycle, and it's a huge issue.

This isn't just coming directly from the political parties, this is coming from their supporters too.

Supporters flock to Twitter to promote their leaders' ideologies, racking up thousands of impressions and quickly sparking the flames within their own small following to ignite a debate that reaches thousands across the globe.

To the individual writing the tweets, it's simply them voicing their opinion no different to how they do in conversation, in actuality it's the equivalent of buying an advert for that political party in the local newspaper.

So where do we go from here? Do we tear down the platforms available to us because of the evil it can commit? Or do we use these same tools that result in so much evil in our world to improve our existence?

The answer to me is obvious. I would much rather live in a world where everyone has a voice than only the rich.

If you're reading this, the likelihood is you're either someone interested in marketing and want to read a book that helps you learn more about this topic, or you're my mum.

Throughout this book I'll be exploring ideas within the industry, brands that have effectively used them, and when a brand has executed its marketing poorly. As you're likely to be reading this and aspiring to find ways of improving your own brand, the book features ideas from the creation of your brand to potentially the future of advertising and what we should expect.

There's something to be learnt from every brand's story, especially if it goes wrong. Even if you begin advertising with the intention of never making any money, understanding how to efficiently promote your ideas, services or products will help you potentially succeed in the future (just don't spend money you don't have).

The greater you understand marketing nowadays, the more control you have in your own future.

I work in marketing, and on a monthly basis am able to look at a variety of different industries and what works best in each one.

From market research and developing new product lines, to simply experimenting with different colours to understand which attracts more clicks; there are a million different factors that contribute to the effectiveness of an advertising campaign within each industry.

It never boils down to simply "If I make the advert pretty, it will work". If that was how advertising worked, the whole industry would be full with art students, and it's not.

Understanding all of the different reasons an individual decided to interact with a brand (purchase from, follow on social media, etc.) allows you to create a recipe that can be replicated and reproduced. As long as the product/service is a decent quality, your knowledge is now a killer asset to both your own future and any other brand that wants to work with you.

Knowledge is ultimately power, and irrelevant of whether you're looking to build your own brand in the future, pursue a career in advertising or looking to have more leverage as an employee.

Gaining a greater understanding of marketing isn't just helpful for people who work in advertising, sales or are business owners; it's also helpful for better understanding every other role within the company.

An employee who doesn't understand their employer's marketing strategy is ultimately missing a lot of key information that could be beneficial within their everyday job. Even something as simple as communicating with customers can be improved with a better understanding of the marketing.

For instance, if I'm targeting tradesmen, they probably won't appreciate the same fluffy, small-talk centric approach that is standard within a 5 star hotel. They (usually) just want the facts, and laid out as quickly as possible.

Better communication means an overall better quality service, and therefore results in improved customer retention.

And if you're improving the company's customer retention and therefore improving revenue, you're much less replaceable than someone that does the bare minimum.

Throughout the book I'll be exploring topics within marketing, and will be looking at companies and individuals that have both succeeded and failed at growth. Whilst I can't cover every company and topic within the industry (because that's impossible), I do think that the ones I've chosen to write about within this book are a great example to study, and generally aren't the stories that other books or films focus on.

Please keep in mind that this book is to be consumed as entertainment, and any shortcuts I've taken explaining a topic are to help the storytelling experience.

Sit back and enjoy, and don't forget to give this book a nice review on Amazon.

THOSE WHO SHOUT LOUDEST

Advertising is now our voice.

The bulk of this book is looking at the commercial application of advertising and marketing. However, I first wanted to write about how advertising techniques are used outside of a commercial setting for other uses such as activism.

As I write this book, protests have formed across the globe following the murder of George Floyd. These protests are promoting the Black Lives Matter movement and seeking to bring justice for the ethnic minorities unfairly targeted by police.

Those involved in this movement have turned to social media to help organise their protests, spread information about current events in real time, and fundraise for Black Lives Matter, the memorial of George Floyd and other organisations.

Recent months have shown that the media are unpredictable with their coverage, and that their truths are unreliable in validity; resulting in social media being the go-to solution for many in order to stay informed.

Not only does this refer to their coverage of the protests and Black Lives Matter recently, but also their coverage of the global COVID-19 pandemic.

Unfortunately it's in times of crisis that we begin to see how bad media bias has become and how often misinformation is presented as fact. Because of this, news about the protests has largely come directly from those on the front-line, organically gaining traction through the public promoting it online.

On Tuesday the 2nd of June, millions across the world posted a black square on their Instagram page for "Blackout Tuesday", which was planned to help spread awareness for the movement and its causes.

Many joined to post the black square, with people of various follower counts (from average citizens to A list celebrities) getting involved to show their support.

This viral advertising campaign for the Black Lives Matter movement is reminiscent of how Fyre Festival advertised their upcoming event by getting influencers to post an orange square on to their profile.

The idea is simple; to disrupt people's scrolling with a block of colour. Unlike most influencer marketing campaigns, everyone involved is posting the same thing as opposed to posing with a product or posting an advert from the brand themselves.

The same logic applies to Blackout Tuesday. By everyone posting a black square together it creates a sense of unity and camaraderie; if you're unaware why people are posting the black square you'll probably look into it to find out more.

Whilst Blackout Tuesday did see huge amounts of people taking part, it wasn't a complete success.

As the campaign was spread via word of mouth rather than one unified organiser, there seems to be inconsistencies on how people posted the square.

Everyone used a black square (good start), but people's captions were an issue. Whilst it seems simple, Blackout Tuesday was actually slightly more complicated than intended.

Many people posting the square used the Black Lives Matter hashtags, resulting in the feeds that were previously vital for organisers to see information about the protests becoming flooded in darkness. Blackout Tuesday unintentionally resulted in an information blackout.

Secondly, many have said that the captions should have featured places where followers can donate or support, which most of the posts I saw did not include.

The campaign was successful in its goal of raising awareness for the movement, but with better organisation and clear advert copy it probably could have raised a substantial amount more money for the causes (in addition to not obscuring protest information).

Social media is becoming a more integral part of organising political movements thanks to the freedom of information on these websites.

The Hong Kong protests throughout 2019 and 2020 (at the time of writing they still are ongoing) found that the Chinese government's global influence meant that information about the protests wasn't reaching the public. Media companies, celebrities and other organisations failed to speak on the matter. Many pointed to China's financial involvement with those who stayed silent.

Similarly to the recent Black Lives Matter protests, those involved in the Hong Kong protests turned to social media to help raise global awareness. They utilised each platform to share news and used encrypted message platforms to communicate with each other without the government being able to see.

These technologies have allowed the average person to have access to a reach that used to be exclusive to the rich and powerful, making protests and political movements spread at a previously impossible pace.

Everyone gets a voice.

It's not just a few individuals with a megaphone that become heard, it's thousands of activists using their platforms to activate their following into taking action.

At its best, it's a revolutionary tool that empowers the public making them heard. At its worst, the same tools can be used to create a mob mentality.

Twitter often becomes the literal court of public opinion, and a prosecution can result in your life being ruined.

Whilst society is progressing socially, the court of public opinion is not.

Journalists have proven themselves unworthy to hold "wrongdoers" in contempt, allowing social media to become the new place for people to be publicly prosecuted and shamed. Social media users move likes hordes, tearing down public perception and providing financial punishment to whomever they see fit.

Realistically, the punishment never truly meets the crime, and the consistency of the court is questionable.

Whether it's James Gunn being fired from his own film series due to jokes from years prior to that series even beginning, or Chris Brown not receiving any punishment despite his (alleged) inability to stop assaulting his girlfriends; trying to understand how social media decides who receives this backlash and who doesn't is an impossible task designed to cause insanity.

The first problem with trying to understand the court of public opinion is that issues are now black and white, there is no longer room for grey. Because of this, social media determines there are two kinds of human; people and nazis.

If you agree with left wing politics, you're a person. If you agree with right wing politics, you're a nazi. According to this logic, there is no central political stance, just right and left. Or, in their opinion, the moral side and the nazis.

That may sound dramatic, but even with the Black Lives Matter protests we see this to be true.

THOSE WHO SHOUT LOUDEST

A photo came out showing a protester hugging a policeman with the caption saying "Solidarity". Following this, someone responded with "Y'all see any pictures of Jewish ppl hugging nazis for peace?" - that tweet currently sits at 350,000 likes, and many have made the same comment across Twitter.

I don't want my stance to be mistaken; I am on the protesters side. However, labelling all the police as being nazis is such a weird blanket statement, and shows that in this person's perspective there is no resolve until everyone on the other side is eradicated. It's also textbook gaslighting, as nobody wants to align with a "nazi".

This divisive logic results in only one side of the political spectrum being heard. This is counterintuitive for political issues as it stops people from being able to create their own opinion, and prevents a two-sided conversation from being had to find resolution.

Most political subjects quickly devolve into absurdity on Twitter, and it's to be expected when you consider that social media often runs on raw emotion.

This raw emotional reaction to every issue mirrors the same irresponsible reporting that resulted in journalists losing their credibility, and what allowed social media to become the new face of public opinion.

THOSE WHO SHOUT LOUDEST

The issues that the court of public opinion deal with aren't black and white, despite how many on social media may represent them. There are grey areas, and as it currently stands these are completely overlooked because there's no reason for them to be exposed. If people were exposed to all sides of a story, we would live in a more empathetic society, but Twitter is designed to be an echo chamber for each user's beliefs.

So what's the difference between irresponsible journalism and social media cancel culture? Money.

When journalists lie and incorrectly accuse someone of a crime, the news agency they work for can potentially face financial repercussions. When thousands of people on social media falsely report on a story, nothing happens.

Eventually someone in power will have misinformation hurt them financially so much that they seek financial repercussions, and that's when things become awkward. Hopefully, the individuals who originally spread the misinformation are held accountable, but there is a chance that the social media platforms will be penalised because of it.

If that happens, the social media platforms will potentially begin to crack down on each individuals' reach.

It would be saddening if these tools that are so empowering for activist movements are taken away because of a small (but very vocal) minority carelessly spreading rumours pretending they're facts.

Access to these tools has become part of our free speech, and it's frightening that they can be taken away.

That being said, I don't see that becoming a reality.

Social media and online marketing is ultimately a good thing in society, even if it has its downsides.

The public now has more power than the media in spreading news, and that expands to promoting the organisations they support too. This has generally made the internet more of a democracy than a dictatorship like the mainstream media had beforehand.

Those who were previously faceless and unheard, now can create an online identity that's known across the globe, and that's pretty amazing.

THOSE WHO SHOUT LOUDEST

Understanding brand identity.

Brand identity is such an interesting concept, because it's essentially your brand's personality.

As someone who writes articles and uploads them to my website, it's very easy to create an identity for my "brand" because it's ultimately just me talking about topics I'm interested in. However this isn't true of everyone who creates content online (obviously).

Whether you've got a Twitter account with 20 followers, or an Instagram account with 200,000; eventually you'll probably do something to increase engagement with your content. You may not even consider what you do on social media to be "content", but it is. Ultimately you're creating something for the entertainment of others, even if nobody actually finds it entertaining.

It could be posting a racy photo to your otherwise PG Instagram profile, or writing a nasty criticism about a newly released album on Twitter; you're intentionally creating content that will probably have a higher engagement due to its "shock factor", even if it's not reflective of your personality in real life.

Likes, replies, comments, follows and shares are currency on social media, which is why we get a dopamine rush when one of our posts gets a larger response than usual. If you get enough of this type of engagement, your personal brand will eventually have a monetary amount assigned to each post, and you might have yourself a career as an "influencer".

The bigger the audience and engagement, the more an influencer can charge per post on their social media account.

Because of this, it's become common for influencers to create content that causes growth even if it's not reflective of the individual's personal values.

As I wrote in my book *The Influencer Bubble*:

> "If you're a Twitter comedian this probably means darker and more controversial jokes. If you're a YouTuber who films themselves travelling, this could mean going somewhere dangerous or where you're not meant to go. If you're a female Instagram influencer, this probably means sexualising your content to grow a male audience.

Not that I'm saying there is anything wrong with capitalising on these things, but when you give up your own personal values in the pursuit of higher earning potential it can be a dangerous path."

It's reported that the average influencer with between 6,000 to 10,000 followers makes an average of $88.00 (£72.00) per post, but the actual monetary amount that a social media account is worth depends greatly on who is following it.

If your following of 6,000 consists entirely of multi-millionaire vintage car collectors, a vintage car dealership will probably spend much more than £72.00 for a post. If you're a savvy influencer, you might even ask for a commission and make a percentage per car you help sell.

The key is utilising your audience to their full potential. If you understand what demographic your audience is, and understand what style of advertisement they respond best to; you can expect to effectively monetise the audience relatively easily.

You shouldn't expect great results if you push a product your audience is unlikely to be interested in. For instance, don't advertise a razor designed for testicles to a predominantly female audience.

THOSE WHO SHOUT LOUDEST

It may sound obvious, but if you look at which brands choose to sponsor which YouTubers, it may surprise you how much of a disconnect there is between the YouTuber and the product they are promoting.

Whilst corporations generally value an influencer or social media account based on its following and engagement, it's not always reflective of the revenue this influencer is capable of generating.

This was seen when Instagram influencer Arii tried to create a clothing brand. At the time, she had over 2,000,000 followers on the platform, giving her the kind of reach that corporations would typically pay at least 5 figures for per post.

The clothes she designed weren't anything offensively bad, but they also weren't eye catching.

Given her massive reach and the amount she likely charges per post, you'd think her clothing brand would hit the ground running almost immediately, and would sell like hotcakes upon release.

Unfortunately, Arii failed to sell the minimum manufacturer's requirement of 36 pieces of apparel, so she technically didn't make any money from her clothing brand.

THOSE WHO SHOUT LOUDEST

There's a lot of reasons Arii probably failed to sell her clothing line, but I think it comes down to the profile's lack of defined demographic.

If your profile is filled exclusively with "timeline filler" such as photos of landscapes, selfies, or jokes; there's very little personality for the audience to connect to.

People may follow or engage with the content because they like looking at the pretty photos or smiling at the jokes, but the lack of identity means they won't likely have a personal connection to the brand.

Identity doesn't necessarily have to relate to connecting to the brand on an emotional level, as it can be based on similar interests.

If you take a look at Dan Bilzerian's Instagram you'd think that his brand of debauchery and excess lacks real substance. But his controversial content attracts those who want to live a similar lifestyle (regardless of how unobtainable or ridiculous that may be). More specifically an audience of predominantly young, male partygoers.

So when he launched his CBD brand, he had millions of young reckless people who wanted to buy the products because it made them feel like they were Dan Bilzerian, even though in reality they're just a college student getting stoned in their room.

The shock value of Dan Bilzerian's brand also resulted in his business getting the kind of exposure organically that other brands are unable to buy.

A similar logic can be applied to creating an identity for any other business or organisation. Depending on the goal of your brand depends on how its identity needs to be formed.

The fashion label Yeezy (by Kanye West) gained a large amount of traction through being polarising in its industry, turning Kanye West's controversial tabloid coverage into billboards for upcoming releases of clothes and footwear.

I imagine that if a charity tried a similar approach, it probably wouldn't receive very many donations.

One of the best examples of a company understanding its industry and finding its identity within it is Gymshark, the English sportswear brand.

In just 8 years, Gymshark has managed to gain enough traction for it to stand toe-to-toe with some of the biggest brands in sportswear. Whilst not an immediate success, the last few years has seen Gymshark grow significantly.

THOSE WHO SHOUT LOUDEST

In the last 6 months (January to June 2020), Gymshark has received more search interest than Reebok in the UK, which has existed for over 60 years and is a solidified name within the athletic community.

Its monumental growth can largely be attributed to its powerful social media advertising and unique brand message.

A quick glance at Gymshark's website probably won't help you differentiate their branding from others. However, a closer look at their advertising and you'll notice that unlike its competitors, Gymshark doesn't have many athletes advertising their products.

Using athletes as "brand ambassadors" has been a tried and tested method of sportswear branding since... well, forever. Nike infamously signed LeBron in a lifetime deal for over $1 billion.

It's a pretty straight forward logic; if athletes use a brand, it's probably the best sportswear for their performance. Wannabe athletes will want to buy the product to try and improve their performance, and sports fans will want to buy the sportswear to look like their favourite athlete.

THOSE WHO SHOUT LOUDEST

It would be pretty difficult for Gymshark to infiltrate the sports community and sign athletes without handing over a hefty amount of money.

Instead, Gymshark focuses on signing influencers, rather than athletes. "Instagram Models", "Fitness Accounts", "Butt Models"; whatever you want to call them, Gymshark loves them.

A huge part of these influencers' content is showing progress pictures, showing their drastic weight loss or muscle "gains". All of their accounts seem to orientate around self-improvement, and by association with this content, Gymshark has become a brand pushing self-improvement.

Athletes talk about breaking records and one upping their competition. Influencers talk about beating their own personal best.

Big sportswear brands want to be associated with the best in the business. Gymshark wants to be associated with the most likeable and relatable fitness personalities on social media.

Because of this, Gymshark is a much more approachable brand for casual gym goers than Nike or Adidas.

People don't feel like they need to be a hardcore weight-lifter to wear Gymshark, whereas buying other sportswear brands when you're only just starting a sport or workout routine often feels daunting, as if you're buying a ticket to join an exclusive club of elite athletes. Some people like the feeling of wearing what a professional athlete does. For many people who are just trying to get into fitness, though, it feels a bit silly.

Also, Gymshark's clothing quality is extremely soft and comfortable, as opposed to being focused on the aerodynamics of the body, making it more enjoyable to wear.

It's this approachability that has made Gymshark successful so far, and that will see it grow even further in the coming years.

Understanding brand identity and how to create something your target audience connects to is essential for the long term success of a brand.

Obviously it's important to make sure a brand isn't too specific or unable to change, as it should be able to grow and adapt depending on what's relevant at that time.

Too many brands today become stagnant and unwilling to change, scared of the potential backlash that comes with it.

They become comfy, happy with how things are and scared of changing in case things then become *less comfy*.

THOSE WHO SHOUT LOUDEST

It's the kind of thinking that results in companies being left in the dust, as more dynamic and young brands begin to approach and overtake them.

This is an issue within every industry at every level, from small local companies to multi-billion pound empires.

Not that Berkshire Hathaway needs a shiny website, but take a look at theirs. They're a multi-hundred-billion dollar company and their website looks like it was designed by a year 7 student learning HTML for the first time.

Luckily for Berkshire Hathaway, I'm sure the sheer amount of money at their disposal makes any advertising pretty irrelevant, but it seems odd that such a prominent business would not want to create a more impressive identity for itself.

If you're in control of a brand or its advertising, you should be able to enjoy that creative freedom for the gift it is.

Creative freedom allows us to experiment and create without the fear of being wrong, because even if something is incorrect it's simply an opportunity to learn and grow.

Online advertising allows for significantly more change in how we express ourselves or advertise. Unless tampering with something is going to significantly damage the livelihoods of others, you should be able to change and adapt it constantly without interference.

Gymshark only succeeded in sportswear because it was bold enough to try something new, rather than trying to copy the formula of a brand from 70 years ago. And every successful influencer nowadays only became so because they weren't scared of other's opinions.

The world isn't written in ink and pencils anymore, and the only time your name is published is no longer in an obituary.

Branding (both for businesses and individuals) is more important than ever, and we're unlikely to go back to a world where that isn't the case. So celebrate your individuality, and ensure you're using it to your benefit.

THOSE WHO SHOUT LOUDEST

Your limitations are a feature, not a bug.

One of the most imposing obstacles about starting or promoting a brand is the limitations you often face.

Whether it's promotional budget, size of service area, amount of staff, or any of other lack of resource; every brand has difficulties when starting out.

When trying to sell a product or service, these limitations often feel like a mountain you have to overcome everyday. Ideally you would have a six figure promotional budget and can achieve a nationwide coverage from your first day operating, but it's rarely the case.

People often forget how difficult it is to advertise an online store, and how many different obstacles there are before making it capable of paying for itself.

Too often will I see business owners think the solution to their financial problems is to have an ecommerce platform made by a website developer for the cheapest price possible, without any real understanding of how ecommerce works or how to effectively market it.

Most of the time when I see this, the product or service they are selling on this platform is identical to what is already available via their competitors who already have considerable amounts more brand awareness online.

Because of this, it becomes a case of *the best price wins*, and when you're going head-to-head with companies like Amazon and other large businesses, it becomes extremely difficult to stay competitive.

Even if the price does edge-out the competition, the website has to be advertised effectively and the online store needs to be designed professionally enough that the potential customer trusts it with their payment information. If the potential customer doesn't trust the website, they simply won't purchase from it.

A good way of instilling trust is through using payment gateways that they already know, such as PayPay. However for small online shops these payment gateways can take a big chunk of the profit that they typically would see if someone was to buy in a bricks and mortar store.

THOSE WHO SHOUT LOUDEST

These issues only worsen when you look at only selling to a limited service area, such as a 10 mile radius from your shop address.

The smaller a service area the less potential customers you're able to reach, resulting in the advertising costs increasing as you fight competition over a limited selection of buyers.

One industry that has been significantly affected by this issue is the UK boiler industry.

Every home needs a boiler, and the local market has quickly become oversaturated with small companies selling boilers. Overall the issue is due to there being too many companies selling the exact same products and forcing the costs of advertising within the heating industry to sky rocket.

Additionally, due to manufacturers giving all of their boiler installers identical tools to market products, the only difference between each local company is their price and how much marketing budget they have.

And this is just one industry example.

So, is it all doom and gloom? No.

Despite the limitations, small businesses do have a better chance of fighting off big competitors than in the past.

THOSE WHO SHOUT LOUDEST

Due to the availability of market research tools such as Google Ads Keyword Planner, Google Trends and Facebook Ads Manager, companies can now carry out extensive market research to better understand the demand and competition within their industry.

Market research should always be an integral part of advertising, and was previously difficult to complete for small companies. Bigger companies can get their thousands of customers to complete surveys, or they can pay marketing agencies to complete research; small companies generally could make educated guesses based on their own intuition and hope they reflect their customer base.

With these research tools we're now able to better understand what exactly potential customers are interested in and plan advertising or products around this. Most of these tools are free, which is also a massive bonus.

Additionally, thanks to online marketing, local companies are now able to better communicate their USPs (unique selling points) to potential customers.

Do you have years of experience within the industry that can help clients find products that will last longer? Tell them! Do you offer something that big companies completely overlook? Promote that!

THOSE WHO SHOUT LOUDEST

Thanks to digital advertising you don't have to rely on flyers or word of mouth to get your USPs seen by a target demographic, you can have them sent directly to their social media accounts or appear in search results for a small advertising budget.

Being small often allows for a better service or product, as you're able to spend more time focusing on each customer and their unique requirements. Being too big often eliminates the reason why people initially liked the brand.

Checkatrade could have this logic applied to their service.

Checkatrade's concept is very simple; advertise trustworthy tradesmen to people looking for them.

Whilst the website is still popular, it's easy to argue that Checkatrade has lost credibility both amongst tradesmen and consumers, thus potentially spelling murky waters in the coming future.

Despite their apparent appeal being the quality of the tradesmen they list, Checkatrade seems more than happy for anyone to join their website, resulting in an oversaturated marketplace.

Even if I narrow my search to be within a mile of my home, there are more tradesmen listed than necessary.

THOSE WHO SHOUT LOUDEST

Without an element of exclusivity, Checkatrade is pretty much identical to any other directory.

In addition to the sheer quantity of tradesmen on Checkatrade, deciphering which are actually worth hiring isn't made any easier by Checkatrade's rating system, which seems to rate everyone above 9/10.

Checkatrade's rating system isn't a particularly fair one, though.

Any reviews that are submitted need to be verified for them to go live, and you can't simply "submit a review" on to a tradesman's page. Additionally, as the review information is submitted to the tradesman directly for their approval, there's pressure on the customer to be more favourable.

As a result, a plumber who is 3 stars on Google (6/10) can get a 10/10 rating on Checkatrade. Or a builder who commonly overpriced work or doesn't complete the job can easily be rated over 9/10 (because they'll cherry pick the reviews left on their profile).

As a result, Checkatrade's ability to keep people using the website after the first time is questionable.

For the tradesmen themselves, Checkatrade continues to be an uphill battle.

THOSE WHO SHOUT LOUDEST

The oversaturated listings combined with the expensive fees has made many tradesmen leave the Checkatrade.

These don't tend to be the "cowboy" tradesmen who are leaving, and are probably those who have a reputation for their quality work elsewhere (or have good marketing outside Checkatrade) so can afford to not be listed.

Checkatrade's entire appeal was that it connected homes with high-quality tradesmen, but by becoming greedy they've destroyed this initial selling point. Instead of being a directory of local high-quality tradesmen, it's just a directory of every tradesmen within the area who have jumped on the Checkatrade band wagon. They've eliminated the exclusivity of their website, taking away its main USP.

Exclusivity is a killer selling point for pretty much every business type.

Of course this is most evident within the fashion industry, which regularly limits the amount of a product released to create a rush of demand. The success of a collection is often measured by how quickly it sells out, rather than the quantity of products sold.

Supreme's releases have become renowned for the literal seconds that they take to sell out completely.

THOSE WHO SHOUT LOUDEST

In the watch world, Richard Mille has become arguably the king of its industry due to focusing on exclusivity and limiting the amount of watches available.

Richard Mille, for those who are unaware, is a luxury watch brand owned by (you guessed it) Richard Mille. His watches are notoriously expensive, with collectors such as Drake boasting several watches by the brand worth well over $750,000 a piece.

Richard could easily build his luxury watch brand to rival Rolex, but he doesn't. He's not interested in chasing the mass appeal of these other high-end brands, mainly because he created his own to avoid the headaches that come with mass production. Instead, Richard focused on the art of creating one of a kind watches.

As a result, the brand attracts serious watch collectors, and increasing the demand within this wealthy demographic has resulted in these watches reaching their current prices.

Stock isn't the only thing you can limit to add value to your brand. Even something as simple as limiting the functionality of a product can result in its appeal increasing.

In a world where apps like Spotify and Tidal have given us the ability to listen to almost every popular artist that has ever lived, people are now beginning to return to cassettes and vinyl.

Even people born after these technologies were the primary listening experience are adopting them due to their novelty factor.

As music streaming platforms are paying artists an abysmal amount for their music (with Spotify currently paying artists $0.00318 per stream at the time of writing), cassettes and vinyls have become a great way for fans to support their favourite artists whilst also having physical collectables. Additionally, these forms of listening are often considered a more intimate way of enjoying the music.

Independent artists and music labels in particular have adopted cassettes, clothing and other forms of merchandise as a way to monetise their passion projects.

Some notable adopters of this revenue stream in the digital age are Odd Future and Chance The Rapper, who initially released all of their music for free on websites like Soundcloud and YouTube whilst making a fortune through selling merchandise and performing shows.

By the time that record labels tried to sign these artists they were already making more money than they ever thought possible through these alternative routes. This empowered them to either force the record labels to give them a huge signing bonus and a fairer contract, or simply keep progressing their career independently.

Simplicity often means less headaches for the brand, irrelevant of what they are creating. The more you try to achieve, the more you have to split your focus, and sometimes this can damage the overall quality of your product/service.

Even in the smartphone industry we're beginning to see brands emerge that are attempting to strip back their devices' capabilities.

The Light Phone was a crowdfunded device released back in 2017 (with the original crowdfunding campaign ending in 2015).

It was created around a very simple concept: smartphones have too many distractions, so the Light Phone won't have any.

The original Light Phone could only make and receive phonecalls. There was no other functionality, it couldn't even text or store contacts.

The Light Phone company then moved on to their second device, the Light Phone 2, which was released in 2019. This device had some more features, including a phonebook, being able to text and an alarm clock. They're looking to introduce more useful features in the coming months, including a taxi app, music and maps.

The phones themselves aren't particularly exciting as devices, the biggest standout property of the phone is its e-ink display that makes it look like a tiny Kindle.

The original phone (in my opinion) made more sense than its sequel, as the original was just for when you want to avoid receiving notifications (going on a walk, at a restaurant, etc.) but want to be contactable in the event of an emergency, whereas the second phone tries to be a standalone device.

Realistically, the Light Phone 2 doesn't really have any benefits over using a basic Nokia. In terms of functionality, the Nokia is almost identical but you can pick one up for £7.50 from Argos.

However, unlike these Nokia phones, the Light Phone 2 gets a lot of buzz from the tech and indie community. And, of course, this is because of their genius branding and advertising.

Looking at the Light company's branding you'd think they were a cutting edge smartphone developer or lifestyle brand. "Designed to be used as little as possible" their website proudly proclaims, over big imagery of landscapes and tranquil settings.

Dumping your smartphone won't automatically make you the type of person who goes for walks or sits in a park and just listens to the wind; but their website makes you think it will.

Their brand and messaging also consistently questions whether smartphones are a positive influence on our lives. It never directly states "our phone will make you happier", but the implication is definitely apparent.

By combining these messages which we usually associate with wellbeing brands and the minimalism we associate with Apple (and other technology brands), Light manages to make an extremely boring device/phone into a fashion statement.

It's this messaging and branding that secured the device over £2.5 million in funding/presales through Indiegogo.

Light and Nokia produce similar devices, but Light manages to make their limited functionality a much more desirable feature for ages between 18 and 30.

It's an impressive case study of how to make something relatively original in an industry where every other brand is making devices that do *everything*, by simply making a device that does *less*.

THOSE WHO SHOUT LOUDEST

Whilst Light are using their devices' minimalism to market to young adults, I've also seen other brands do so targeting older markets.

One newspaper advert I came across was advertising simplistic unbranded flip phones (which they probably just bought through Alibaba).

The advert featured this hilarious quote "Mum and Dad said 'We ONLY want to make PHONE CALLS, not tweet our lives away!'"

The key selling point for these flip phones was that they are "Easy to use" and had "No Internet, No Wi-Fi, No GPS, and No Games".

So considering you can get a similar phone with more features for £7.50, how much do you think this unbranded flip phone cost? £10, £20, maybe even £30 at a push?

Nope, they priced it as £79.95 (which apparently included a £30 discount). By tailoring the advert towards an older generation who won't be looking online for cheaper alternatives, they're able to make the device massively overpriced.

Exploitative or genius? I guess it depends who you ask.

THOSE WHO SHOUT LOUDEST

As technology becomes more complicated, I think the value of simplicity will continue to increase. Consumers want things to be simple because they don't want hassle. The more straight-forward using or purchasing a product is, the quicker that person can actually enjoy it.

A good example of a company that has also focused on minimalising an experience in a more traditional industry is Boxt, who are a heating company and boiler installer in the UK.

I used to do online marketing for a local heating engineer who installed, serviced and repaired Worcester Bosch boilers. Throughout the year Worcester Bosch would send recommendations for improving the client's marketing, and one of their favourite companies to use as a shining case study of "who is doing it right" was Boxt.

Boxt, at the time, was a trailblazer in the industry. They appeared out of nowhere and were growing like wildfire, with their coverage quickly expanding across the South of England, and then to its current national coverage.

Within a year Boxt had become the second largest installer of boilers in the UK, installing over 4,000 boilers and generating over £18 million in sales revenue (information taken from

Zone Digital's PDF case study of Boxt for The Marketing Society's new brand award nomination).

So what did they do differently?

Before Boxt arrived, if you wanted a new boiler installation you had to phone a local heating engineer and schedule a home appointment for them to provide a quote. A heating engineer would come to take all the relevant information about your home, and would then sell you a boiler that met your unique requirements.

Boxt worked differently, eliminating this process by offloading it on to their website.

Their intuitive website asks the customer for the information that the heating engineer would usually collect, and then asks for their postcode. Immediately the website is able to provide a variety of different boiler quotes, varying in price and brand. Each boiler has its own unique page giving you all of its specifications and features, allowing you to make an educated decision on which will best suit your home.

Then, if you find one you like the look of with a price that sounds right, you can immediately book an engineer to come install the boiler.

Better yet, Boxt's quotes were generally much cheaper than your average heating engineer, sometimes almost £1,000 less. This was thanks to Boxt cutting out the sales process of going to customers' homes. And if you can't afford the installation price, Boxt allows you to spread the cost into monthly instalments with finance.

Thanks to the website being able to provide a quote and also schedule the installation appointment in one system, receiving a new boiler was as easy as ordering a phone case from Amazon.

Most other local plumbing and heating companies were focusing on implementing different services to try and spread their net as far as possible, whereas Boxt was simply focused on creating the best experience possible with one service.

Boxt is now a big name in its own right and its boiler booking system has been copied by thousands of companies across the UK, but they are the only one that has dominated the industry so effectively.

I think the key takeaway from Boxt's success is that if you're able to improve an essential service for potential customers, they'll probably be interested in using it.

It's worth mentioning that Boxt didn't just catapult to be king of the boiler industry simply due to their website, despite how revolutionary it may be for the industry.

There was a lot of clever marketing to make the website gain traction, along with a lot of smart business moves that helped them grow a network of boiler installers across the UK to help carry out the work.

So keep in mind that yes, a good idea is always worth pursuing, but its success may not be immediate.

THOSE WHO SHOUT LOUDEST

Your limitations are probably not that big anyway...

Whilst it may seem intimidating comparing yourself to other established companies within your industry, things are probably not as bad as they first seem.

Many of the limitations that typically stunted brands in the past are now beginning to become a smaller concern.

With the current graphic design tools available, brands are able to launch products without needing to pay for them to be manufactured.

Over the last couple of years I've been helping a client build a furniture company. One of the most intriguing things about the brand's initial launch was the lack of product imagery we were working with.

Of the 9 products initially featured on the website, we had only produced 5 of them. 2 of those 5 products had been created only once prior to the brand launch. Despite this, the website was full of images showing each product in various styles and in different projects. We did this by creating photorealistic renders, as opposed to manufacturing the products and taking photos of them.

Following the launch, I began to notice how many other brands have done exactly the same thing and it surprised me.

For example, a lot of the photos on IKEA's website may look like real rooms they've created, but the majority of these images are renders.

Whilst an initially scary concept for consumers, the possibilities that these images create for aspiring business owners is infinite.

If you're interested in creating and selling a product, it's easier than ever. Not only do you save costs on manufacturing, but this also helps reduce the upfront commitment of potentially paying for a bulk amount of your products to be created with no way of knowing if they'll sell.

Instead, you can simply render the product (making sure the design can be manufactured) and market it, testing if it will sell enough to mass produce and judging how consumers react to the product.

THOSE WHO SHOUT LOUDEST

This is an important tool for helping growing brands create a more complete catalogue of products without needing to mass produce them and then pay for storage whilst trying to generate sales.

Instead, they can advertise the products and manufacture upon selling an item.

If you think that customers may be put off by the long wait times to receive the items (due to each item being manufactured upon purchasing), simply create a form so people can enquire and you can communicate the wait time to them. If you get lots of enquiries and people say the wait time is too long, you will know that there is enough demand for the product and that keeping a surplus in stock will help sales.

Taking form entries instead of immediate payment generally is a good way of increasing a new brand's sales, especially if you're advertising expensive products.

If people aren't familiar with your brand but want to make an order, they're more likely to leave their details into a form than to provide payment details and pay upfront for a product. By following up on these form entries, you're able to instil trust into your brand and assure people that they're not sending their money to a random bank account in South America.

Similarly, Facebook allows for you to create adverts that connect potential customers directly with your WhatsApp or Messenger account.

People can see an advert for your product or service, and simply click on them to begin messaging your brand.

This is extremely useful as it allows you to have a conversation with the customer as opposed to sending them to a website. That way, if they have any questions about the product, they can ask you directly as opposed to them trying to find the information on their own.

It's not a perfect solution by any means, but for small local brands this is a very effective advertising solution as it reflects the personality and helpfulness that your customers enjoy.

It's amazing how powerful these affordable tools can be at our disposal.

In the right hands, these advertising platforms can deliver the kind of promotion that would traditionally cost millions of pounds.

At the beginning of 2019 a startup called Væv emerged and got massive coverage across the media.

THOSE WHO SHOUT LOUDEST

The company was allegedly selling dirty tissues for people to sniff; thus strengthening their immune system through forcing the user to become exposed to disease. Each tissue was being sold for $80, and by the time it received mass coverage they had already sold out.

The problem is, Væv never existed, and was actually just an elaborate joke in a Comedy Central show. The brand was created to poke fun at how good marketing can make any product appeal to an audience, even if it's a terrible idea.

The branding was designed to be a parody of popular health and wellness brands like Goop, which often receives criticism for being the modern day equivalent of a snake oil salesman.

The name Væv is the Danish word for tissue. When creating the brand, the comedian decided to mimic the same method that the ice cream brand Häagen-Dazs used for creating theirs. The idea being that by using a danish sounding name the brand seems more fancy, even though it's not produced in Denmark.

Even the minimal packaging was a parody of companies like Apple, complete with stickers featuring the logo and the clever slogan "blessed you".

After creating a slick website featuring some impressive high-res photography, a few clever social media accounts, creating a mockup of the product, and conducting some market research they were able to prove that people would use a dirty tissue as an alternative to the flu vaccine.

Additionally, the comedian wanted to expose how gullible journalists can be, and succeeded amazingly.

The company's CEO didn't exist, the company wasn't registered anywhere, there was no record of actual sales or customers; yet the mainstream media jumped on the story immediately.

The Guardian, CNET, Fox News, the New York post and many others wrote stories reporting on the brand. All doing enough research to disprove that the tissues are an effective alternative to the flu vaccine, but not enough to realise that the company and its founder were completely fabricated.

The lack of research into Væv demonstrates how journalists act nowadays, writing whatever will engage audiences and releasing it as quickly as possible (or risk being beaten to the story by competition). If this comes at the cost of research and fact checking, so be it.

TIME did an interview with the brand's imaginary CEO, and within that interview claimed that over 1,000 tissues had been sold. Whilst in the article they did mention that they struggled to find information about the CEO or the company, they seem to pass this off as being a bit bizarre, rather than saying that the brand wasn't real.

Maybe they did think this was fake, but they failed to make this clear. Or, if they did think so, they should have simply not published the articles.

Journalists are meant to uphold the moral standards of society. One of these standards being that they reveal the truth when others don't, yet this didn't happen with Væv.

Of course, they weren't providing positive feedback within their news stories. However, the massive coverage of Væv only resulted in more people wanting to purchase the tissues.

If this wasn't simply a silly skit for a TV show and was indeed someone looking to make a quick buck from selling dirty tissues from their home, the media made it possible for that to happen.

The press coverage resulted in the imaginary company looking established to the general public. Before the media picked up the story, it was just a cool looking website. After they picked it up, it was a real health and wellness business that were selling flu vaccine alternatives.

Væv received the kind of global brand awareness that other startups spend millions attempting to receive, with their brand being covered by a countless amount of news networks and journalists.

The total budget for Væv was $1,000 and one week of time, which is typically a very constricting budget and timeframe.

Comedy Central didn't sell any, but the media's reporting resulted in Væv getting requests to preorder the next batch of tissues (including one for a toddler) via email. If Væv was a real business, the media would have been responsible for the product selling.

I think it's ironic that the same media companies that house the journalists that reported on Væv also consistently criticise websites such as Google or Facebook for their advertising platforms. I understand why they make the criticisms, but evidently these companies are often more responsible and careful with their power than the media.

Væv is an impressive case study of how effectively a small budget can be used to generate huge results.

In the TV show and across media coverage the skit has been dumbed down to make it funnier and more entertaining, but the ideas behind it definitely came with years of knowledge analysing the health and wellness industry.

THOSE WHO SHOUT LOUDEST

I'm not saying you need that level of knowledge to get started, but you definitely shouldn't expect to be on the news across the world in only a week like Væv. Especially if your budget is just $1,000 and you only have a week to make it work (which was the constraints within the show).

The best way to begin building knowledge is through experience.

The comedian who created Væv previously worked within advertising, and all of the skills they collected on their journey would have helped contribute to the success of that viral moment.

If you're hesitant about starting something because of fear of failing, understand that the only way to overcome that feeling is to power through and face failure as it comes.

THOSE WHO SHOUT LOUDEST

Find goals that are relevant to your brand.

Thanks to the technologies available nowadays, there are a huge amount of metrics you can measure success by.

The concept of success varies from person to person, and from brand to brand; and it really depends on what you're looking to achieve or what you perceive the end goal to be.

On a personal level I find it interesting talking to people about how they measure their individual success or what gives them the most pride.

When I was younger, I was confident that success was primarily based on a monetary amount, but with time it seems to change depending on the people I meet and how success has shaped their personality.

To me, the measurement of how successful I am at the moment is based on how content I am with life. If I have no financial worries, am generally feeling fulfilled with my career but not overwhelmed, have a nice home, and feel like my social life is giving me some personal value; I generally feel like I'm as successful as I want to be.

I know plenty of people who don't care about those things, and base their success on different measurements like whether they have a nicer car than you, or on other things like engagement on social media. That's fine, but I'm not going to get stressed chasing those same goals.

If being an influencer is an eventual career goal, it's fine to be concerned with things like post engagement, views and follower count (in moderation). However, if you're obsessing over those things with no intention of making a career out of them, what value are you actually gaining from that experience?

I watched an interesting video recently where a woman used her male friend's photos on Tinder and tried to arrange as many dates as possible within one week (the video was by Alexander Grace).

She decided to take it seriously and only match those who she actually thought he would find attractive, as opposed to simply attempting to focus on sheer quantity of dates.

By day 5 she found that she was struggling to find matches, and when a match did happen she rarely felt like they were interested because they weren't reciprocating the same energy she was sending them.

She said that she felt "down" despite the profile she was using not even being her own, and felt like the experience "was not very healthy", commenting that she thought that if this was an ongoing daily experience there would be some "psychological effects".

I felt similarly when using those apps, feeding way too much into these strangers' opinions of me and whether they found my personality attractive.

Ultimately, it's all irrelevant in the grand scheme of life, and the feeling of inadequacy that comes from measuring yourself to the impossible standard of being *perfect* isn't worth whatever your end goal of using the app is.

That can apply to Instagram which measures people similarly to Tinder, Twitter where you're expected to have exactly the same political opinions as everyone you follow or follows you, or even a gaming platform like Twitch where people may mock your ability to play a game.

Social media is largely based on the dopamine rushes of having people engage with you, and unless you're very strategic about how you use them (such as if you're doing it professionally or use them in moderation) it's very easy to become obsessed with getting that dopamine rush.

That addiction to engagement definitely isn't exclusive to social media either.

As consumers and businesses alike move further on to the internet, brands have begun to adapt their metrics in an attempt to better measure their successes and failures.

There are many metrics used by companies to measure success. In modern business the concept of simply "making money" isn't necessarily a good enough gauge for how successful your business is, as some of the most successful and innovative companies don't turn a profit.

Because every business measures their success by their own methods, it results in a lot of confusion in what to focus on when advertising.

Brand awareness is one focus which probably causes the most confusion.

Do you measure brand awareness by how many people have been reached by an advert? How many times the advert was seen? Or the amount of engagement it had?

In most cases, the default answer is all of the above. As a result, advertising agencies are encouraged to focus on maximising these metrics' numbers as opposed to ensuring that the advert is shown to the most relevant demographic.

As a result, only measuring brand awareness on the amount of people seeing the advert is generally counterintuitive, as it encourages sacrificing accuracy for reach.

Additionally, the accuracy of these metrics is debatable, especially following Facebook's controversy in 2018 regarding "faking video views" (where views were bloated as the app was counting anyone who scrolled by as a video view).

Because of this, never rely solely on one metric for measuring the success of your campaign, and try to find a way of measuring its success that is unique for your company.

Each advertising campaign you launch should have its own goal with its own gauge of success, and these should then accumulate and contribute towards your company's overall marketing goals.

There's nothing wrong with looking at metrics to help recognise change or better understand your advertising, but it's unwise to only focus on the metrics and not the advertising's overall impact on your marketing.

For example, if your bounce rate increases (which is generally bad), but the amount of leads/purchases you receive has gone up; it probably means that your landing page is hyper-focused on the kind of content that your potential customers want to see, helping filter out people who probably won't convert into customers.

If you were to focus on the bounce rate, though, you'd probably think the advert was a failure and restructure it, which would be detrimental to the overall effectiveness of the marketing campaign.

Many brands (usually startups) have begun adopting an intense growth business model.

In the iconic 2015 movie Steve Jobs, the legendary CEO compares his company "NeXT" to an unmanned satellite called Skylab. NASA sent the satellite believing that by the time it entered back into the atmosphere they would have a plan to ensure it crashed safely, but they failed. Luckily it crashed in the sea without an issue, but it could have been catastrophic.

Similarly, Steve started NeXT without a functioning product, hoping that by the time his product came to launch the technology would catch up with his ideas. It didn't, but NeXT was acquired by Apple and therefore was a success (despite its only product launch being a flop).

This is similar to how many startups are operating; recklessly launching their services or products with no clue how to make them profitable, hoping that they somehow figure out how to land on their feet.

The focus is rapid growth, usually with the following plan:

1. Create a free product/service, or if it's not free make it as cheap as possible.
2. Receive funding from a venture capital firm or angel investor.
3. Use the majority of this funding to grow a user base with a vague plan to introduce a profitable service/product to these users later (making the company theoretically worth more than any other non-profitable business).

Also, for good measure, add spending unnecessary money on office space and employees to create the illusion of a successfully growing brand.

Then, after you've drawn out this process as long as possible, the fourth step is to introduce your magic service/product. Usually, though, this service/product is not received by the user base particularly well (because the majority of users only got the service/product because it was cheap or free, not because they intend to spend actual money on it). By this point, the running costs of the startup have bloated so much that even if some of their users do adopt the profitable service/product, it's not enough to sustain the company into the future.

This is one of the key reasons I dislike business models that prioritise growth in users, as it never provides a real reflection of a company's success, and is usually just a way for businesses or marketing agencies to create the illusion of positive growth.

I recently saw a YouTube video by a successful startup creator explaining how the startup industry is becoming a pyramid or ponzi scheme.

In his opinion, the growth focused business model is pushed by early investors of a brand. This then creates the illusion of a prospering company, helping them sell shares to other investors in order to make a return on their initial investment.

This makes sense, and as we see more notable startups fall it begins to become more apparent.

THOSE WHO SHOUT LOUDEST

In 2019, 553 startups failed with a total funding of $1.9 billion going down the toilet. Many of the biggest names in that figure were focused on the initial growth of their brand.

Is the growth model really working? Or is it just implemented in order to create false valuations?

It's not always a bad concept to focus on growing a following before a product launch, of course. The key is context.

For instance, if an influencer or another social media based brand begins trying to push products when they only have 10 followers, they'll probably struggle to grow their following and/or make the social media account profitable.

If you ignore making money from the social media account and focus on releasing content to grow your audience, you'll be able to make far more money in the long-run.

As I mentioned earlier in the book, though, it's important to remember that follower count isn't always reflective of potential sales unless it's created around a particular demographic's common interests.

Similarly to growing a social media following, if you advertise your brand's products prior to release and people subscribe via email for updates on the upcoming launch, it's probably going to be beneficial to the sales of that product at launch.

The issue is when a brand becomes obsessed with the amount of subscribers or followers they have, rather than using it as a tool for advertising and sales.

With the introduction of finance and "buy now pay later" purchasing options, even sales and store purchases have become a muddied metric.

Too often will I see companies plug these loan options into their business as a way of boosting immediate sales, but I don't believe it's the magic solution others hail it as.

I have a few issues with the finance and small loan industry.

Firstly, the business model is designed to take advantage of financially unstable impulse buyers, and can have long term negative effects on their credit score.

Secondly, companies don't necessarily do a background check on consumers, creating a *loan shark esque* business model. They don't care who they're selling to or if they can afford it, but if that person misses payment the consequences can be awful for their long term financial future.

When working for a company who offered finance options for their product I was able to see what information was required before that person was accepted for finance, and I was pretty shocked at how bare the requirements were.

I understand that finance is generally a small amount per month, but if someone has several items on finance it can add up to a substantial amount. On the system I used (which I can't *expose* as it could result in legal issues), it didn't seem to cross-reference each person's financial status or their existing items on finance.

Hairdresser who makes £14k a year? Sure, you can afford a new German sports car! Recruitment consultant earning £22k paying £1,000 in rent a month? Yes, of course you can have a luxury watch!

Most of these businesses that offer finance or "buy now pay later" loans don't adhere to the same standards as banks, which is slightly worrying.

Whilst I understand that it's up to individuals to decide what they can and cannot afford, the 2007 mortgage crisis proved that it's ultimately dangerous to be so generous when approving loans.

Following the housing crisis, banks have tightened their loaning considerably. However, businesses haven't, thus allowing these purchasing options to come into popularity.

Maybe the future will see more regulations or maybe it won't, but I don't see this sales solution having longevity. As we saw with the housing crisis, eventually people begin missing payments in the masses, and when that happens the whole business begins failing as a result.

If you own a company and are considering finance, be careful. This isn't necessarily the "missing piece" that will result in long-term success, and if anything is a short-term game plan implemented to help boost sales.

A lot of industries are now relying on finance to keep them afloat, so I don't want to paint it in too negative a light, but I think you understand my concerns.

So, if you can't focus on sales or users to set goals, what do you do?

As mentioned earlier, every advertising campaign should have its own set of goals based on your brand's unique requirements.

Traffic to your website, amount of people reached, leads, sales, purchases, subscribers, followers, and so on; each advertising campaign goal should be centred around improving a metric that your brand sees value in.

For example, if you're a company that is generating £500k a year on Amazon but making less than £5k on their own website, focusing on improving sales from the company's website would be wise. Otherwise, if Amazon decides one day that they want to create a product range that rivals yours, they could completely destroy your main source of revenue.

Sure, in theory that company would probably want to double down on their advertising on Amazon because the initial results are better. But in actuality you're better off spending that money strengthening your other sales platforms and having more control over where your customers purchase from.

On a similar note, many small restaurants/takeaways who sell on food delivery apps/websites frequently find themselves being charged more and more by these platforms. Because the food delivery marketplace knows that the majority of the orders come directly from them, they can then force the restaurant to pay whatever number they decide or threaten to drop them from the platform (which could result in their orders shrinking significantly).

A lot of these websites/apps will also supply the restaurant with a website within their monthly charges. Whilst it seems like a kind gesture at first, this allows the food delivery app/website to have complete control over that restaurant's online presence.

If that restaurant decides they no longer want to pay the monthly prices, that food delivery app/website then has the power to essentially make them disappear online, potentially resulting in a substantial loss in revenue.

Because of this, I'd always encourage people to own their website themselves, and to avoid using those apps when possible. It's important to build your own platform for connecting to customers, otherwise your company's future is potentially not in your hands.

This is why a company like Tesla has a much higher valuation than many of its competitors despite its smaller sales.

Tesla has control of the production of their cars, doesn't require much advertising spend due to them having such significant brand following, and is developing its own technologies that other car brands will likely want to purchase; resulting in its perceived worth being greater than other brands who sell a larger amount of vehicles.

Its other competitors largely outsource elements of their manufacturing and technology development, thus having less control over their product.

The greater control you have over your brand and its products, the more that brand is valued.

It's easy to become caught up with numbers and allow them to dictate your brand, but in actuality they shouldn't dictate your decisions or how you act.

Even with my own book releases I found myself obsessing over the numbers and where my books land on the charts.

My first release was a guide to help people better understand market research and other elements of marketing, and that book's physical version didn't even touch the charts.

My second release (which is about the influencer industry) peaked at number 47 on Amazon.co.uk's chart for books about advertising.

Later my first book's Kindle version did manage to peak at number 9 on the "Web Marketing" chart, which was a significant jump and largely due to interest in my second release causing a sudden influx of sales.

In terms of monetary value, the charts don't really mean much. Being on the best seller charts didn't even contribute to the majority of the money made on the books, which came from slow and consistent purchases across the space of 3 months.

Sure enough, I'll probably find myself watching where this newest release lands, even if it doesn't actually mean anything significant in the long run.

If I was looking at how to make my books a more consistent form of revenue I'd focus on the unit of sales rather than the peak chart position. This would mean a larger focus on the overall marketing of the book from a day-to-day basis, rather than its immediate kickback.

Realistically it depends on what I'm aiming to achieve.

If I'm writing and releasing books because I enjoy doing it and having people seeing my work, I should keep my current goals, revising each release's success and trying to implement improvements for the next.

If I want to try making it into a career, I'd need to completely rethink my strategy.

I would probably need to plan the book much more rigorously. Researching what topics are the hottest within the advertising industry currently, and analysing the competition to help determine the topic that will receive the most interest.

I'd also need to make sure I find an untouched niché, so my book has a good USP.

I'd then have to write the book as quickly as possible. If the book takes too long to write, people will potentially have moved on to the next *big thing*, or someone else might beat me to publishing a book about it.

I would also need to make sure the book is as long as possible to help justify a price over £10, otherwise the amount made per book won't be close to covering the time spent writing. By making the book more expensive, I'd also be able to expand my distribution beyond Amazon.

Then, once the book is released (or maybe before if I can get pre-orders), I'd need to have a comprehensive marketing plan that results in large and consistent daily sales.

Finally, I'd need to use social media much more effectively, building an audience who would be interested in my website and books as opposed to just consisting of people I know.

Assuming that all goes to plan, I would then be in a position to make writing a proper career path.

Writing probably isn't the best example because it's not the easiest industry to infiltrate, but the message remains the same; find goals that fit your brand, and then create a strategy to achieve them.

Experiment with ideas, services, products & messaging.

My favourite brands to work with are those where I find opportunities to experiment with new ideas.

Being dynamic and capable of adapting products and/or services is important for forward thinking brands, otherwise you can easily become stagnant and unable to grow in any substantial way.

I mentioned it in the *brand identity* chapter, but a lack of change usually results in being overtaken by newer, more adaptable brands.

Take Blockbuster, who were largely considered the king of home video content back in the mid 2000s. Blockbuster, for those who have somehow forgotten or were too young to remember, were a DVD and VHS rental store.

THOSE WHO SHOUT LOUDEST

At its peak it employed almost 85,000 people across the globe, and really felt like the McDonalds of home entertainment.

Over the years Blockbuster seemed to just exist like a library for DVDs, VHS and video games; updating each store's catalogue but not really doing much more aside from that.

Meanwhile Netflix, who offered a similar service to Blockbuster but were much smaller, was experimenting moving their services online. Despite their initial digital library of content seeming tiny in comparison to what was available physically, the online option quickly gained traction.

Unsurprisingly, Blockbuster fell by the wayside, as Netflix became the new king of home entertainment.

Hindsight is 20:20 and looking back it seems shortsighted of Blockbuster to downplay the significance that the internet would play in video, but realistically it's difficult to tell what ideas will or will not pan-out in the future.

For instance, take Spectacles, which is Snap Inc's first attempt at venturing outside of social media (Snap Inc own Snapchat).

THOSE WHO SHOUT LOUDEST

The story begins with Snap Inc acquiring a hardware company called Vergence Labs.

Vergence Labs had developed sunglasses that could record videos in the viewing perspective of the user (the video would record as if you were watching through the user's eyes). Unlike most wearable cameras, the camera within these sunglasses was barely noticeable, helping the video be more authentic and natural for capturing a moment.

Vergence Labs' end goal was to make Augmented Reality (AR) glasses, which would allow the user to see and interact with digital objects through the glasses' lenses.

The video functionality was just the first step towards this goal. As their development team was relatively small, they needed to focus on creating a releasable product which would then help them fund their research into creating AR glasses.

They never achieved augmented reality, as their company was acquired by Snap Inc following the release of their sunglasses, which caught their attention. Snap Inc then refocused their team to focus on the video functionality of their eyewear.

The improved video capability and the bold new design of the sunglasses made them a striking product, and Snap Inc dubbed the eyewear "Spectacles".

The design of the eyewear was unique, and leaned into the "hipster" fashion trends that were popular in 2016. Making the Spectacles attractive to wear was definitely important for making them successful.

Snap Inc even created a popup vending machine for selling the Spectacles called "Snapbot" which had an equally vibrant visual design; appearing like something out of a '70s sci-fi movie mixed with a minion from the film Despicable Me.

The Snapbot would temporarily appear at random locations across the U.S. for people to buy Snapchat Spectacles, with many gathering at the vending machines and forming huge queues to buy their own.

The limited time for making a purchase along with only being able to purchase at the Snapbot resulted in Spectacles gaining a huge amount of hype. Snap Inc perfectly managed to utilise "fear of missing out" to make the illusive Spectacles the most talked about new technology on social media and in the tech news during its initial release.

Snap Inc definitely aren't the first Silicon Valley brand to venture into AR glasses. Google had attempted this with their project Glass, but they never really succeeded at marketing to the general public due to the glasses looking so ridiculously ugly. Google then decided to focus on its commercial application, which seems to be more effective.

Spectacles, though, have mass appeal. They look fun, appealing to a generation of young adults who regularly make video content to share with their friends.

Resale values for the glasses were, of course, massive.

Snap Inc hadn't just created a cool bit of tech, they'd created a fashion statement. The initial buzz of the Spectacles was comparable to a YEEZY or Supreme release, rather than anything you'd expect from a camera company.

And by the looks of it, Snap Inc thought they'd just created the next iPod.

I think it's important that you understand what Vergence Labs were initially aiming to achieve, as it's a big part of why the tech community were originally intrigued by Snap Inc's move into hardware.

Snap Inc purchasing an augmented reality company and then doing mysterious popup releases across the US seemed like the start of something massive; as if the glasses were going to be part of a bigger technological event that was just on the horizon.

With the popularity of Snapchat at the time being unrivalled, it seemed as if Snap Inc were the company who could instruct that kind of huge movement in both the software and hardware industries.

However, that technology wasn't there, and in actuality Spectacles were closer to a sunglasses brand than a revolutionary tech startup.

Which was fine, and they were definitely fashionable sunglasses. The process of buying Spectacles in itself was exciting enough to keep consumers intrigued. The limited availability of the Spectacles also worked in their favour.

However, without the ability to provide a groundbreaking device, Spectacles weren't going to get a huge amount of orders. Spectacles would peak as a fashion statement, and if Snap Inc realised this they would have been able to make Spectacles a much more successful brand.

Snap Inc decided to move their sales from physical (through the Snapbot) to their website. The aim was obviously to launch Spectacles to the masses, hoping the huge demand they saw at the Snapbot would maximise on the internet.

THOSE WHO SHOUT LOUDEST

The distinction between whether Spectacles was a fashion or tech brand is important in this context, as it determines how many units of Spectacles that Snap Inc should make available during this initial release.

If it's a fashion statement, Snap Inc should do limited releases in order to quickly sell out and allow them to continue nurturing the demand of the sunglasses. The fashion route would also allow them to collaborate with other brands for unique spins on the Spectacles design and colour options (like sneaker brands do).

If it's a tech release, Snap Inc should allow for the maximum amount of units to be sold. They should also provide annual releases with the newest iteration of the hardware.

Snap Inc decided to go with the tech release, which was the wrong decision.

They greatly overestimated the demand of the Spectacles, apparently having to write off $40,000,000 worth of unsold hardware.

The irony was that they actually sold 220,000 units, which shows there was good demand for the product. If they had released small quantities of the glasses (and especially if they worked with other fashion brands), Spectacles would have been a monumental success.

Due to the Spectacles only being annual releases and being treated like a technology brand, it quickly lost traction and now only receives 1% of the attention it did at its peak back in 2016.

Snap Inc are continuing to work towards the original vision of Augmented Reality devices, but whether they will be able to achieve this goal with interest dwindling in Spectacles is questionable.

To me, it looks like Snap Inc completely misunderstood their market. If they better utilised their ability to create a fashion brand, it would have resulted in a much stronger brand overall and generated much more revenue for funding their eventual goal of Augmented Reality glasses.

However, if you look at industry trends back in 2016 you would think that Snap Inc were actually making a calculated decision that would have paid off by now.

At the tail end of 2016, VR (virtual reality) headsets began booming in popularity, with many gamers thinking that VR headsets would be widely adopted within the following few years.

So, based on that, you'd think Snap Inc's decision to focus on the potential of Augmented Reality would tie in to that trend.

Whilst there was speculation around whether VR was just a gaming fad, the general consensus was that it was here to stay, especially with so many companies investing billions into the hardware.

Whilst those technologies still exist, they definitely aren't something you expect to see in everyone's living room.

There's still time for these technologies to be widely accepted, but Spectacles are still working towards developing Augmented Reality glasses and until they achieve this and the market for those glasses emerges, we can't expect Snap Inc's big bet to pay off.

It's common for companies in tech to experiment with different services or product ranges with various results, and almost expected of them.

It seems the tech industry believes that diversification is key for brand longevity, and it's arguably something that other industries undervalue.

Sometimes side-projects can overtake the main focus of a business, as was the case for Twitter, which was initially just a throw away side-project by the company/website Odeo.

THOSE WHO SHOUT LOUDEST

Odeo was a podcasting website, but found itself vulnerable once Apple began to infiltrate the podcasting industry by allowing podcasts to be hosted on iTunes in 2005.

As iPods were so popular at this time and were quickly becoming people's favourite way of consuming audio content, Odeo knew its platform was going to be made redundant. Because of this, they tasked their employees to begin conceptualising projects that could become the lifeboat to their sinking ship.

Twitter, then named "twttr", was one of these projects. The website concept wasn't quite what Twitter is today, as it was just an SMS (text message) service that would allow you to send a text to a group of contacts.

Using text messages as an alternative to social media may seem strange in 2020, but back in 2006 social media wasn't widely adopted on mobile devices, so an SMS text service like this filled a gap in the market.

These text message "status updates" would also appear on Twitter's website. The SMS feature would only be deleted in 2019 following it being exploited and Jack Dorsey's (CEO and original developer of Twitter) account being hacked.

THOSE WHO SHOUT LOUDEST

On release Twitter was largely dismissed as a misstep for Odeo, and the media were generally confused at why a podcasting website decided to launch the service.

However, despite this, Odeo continued to support the project.

Twitter's functionality at the time began to become clear when there was a small earthquake in San Francisco and Twitter was used to broadcast the news by its users. Because of this, the company began to rethink the service as an information sharing platform, rather than simply social media.

Twitter would use this new direction during a tech conference (South by Southwest Interactive), placing large TV screens in the corridors featuring status updates about the event.

During this conference, Twitter usage tripled as conversations transferred to the website.

This was largely considered the tipping point for Twitter, kickstarting its growth.

Since then, Twitter has grown to become a social media juggernaut, but it's also an important part of breaking news.

When a plane crash landed in the Hudson River in 2009, a Twitter post broke the news story.

THOSE WHO SHOUT LOUDEST

President Trump and other politicians have adopted Twitter as their way of speaking directly to the public, as opposed to relying on the media. Which, you could argue, isn't always the smartest decision for them.

Twitter regularly finds itself as a centrepiece in breaking news stories, with videos and information spreading rapidly across the globe. Of course, it's not all sunshine and rainbows, as Twitter's ability to spread information (or potentially misinformation) has also made it largely considered the literal court of public opinion, fuelling modern day "cancel culture".

It's amazing to consider that something as integral as Twitter was originally just a small side-project at a podcasting website.

Personally, I had never heard of Odeo, which as of 2017 no longer exists and its website domain has since been sold.

Creating a spin-off brand isn't the only way you can experiment. Ideally, you'll be able to simply expand your offerings under one brand name, rather than having a separate name for each new venture.

THOSE WHO SHOUT LOUDEST

The reason why Twitter needed its own branding was because it was something new and unique, otherwise people would assume it tied into Odeo's website and services.

Brand awareness and repetitive messaging is often vital for the success of a marketing campaign.

Of course you can experiment with new messaging, but if your brand has found success with using a particular voice or approach, maybe don't go in the opposite direction. Especially if it will probably polarize your audience or customers.

A good case study of a brand mismanaging their messaging is the British Army's recruitment adverts in 2018.

"Your country needs you", "I want you for U.S. Army"; advertising so iconic and timeless that the WWI posters are probably vivid in your thoughts.

There are a million reasons why they were so effective, but one is undeniable; it's inclusive. There's no explanation of why the Army needs you – that's for you to decide – but by simply speaking directly to audiences the Army makes us feel like heroes.

I mention this because it explains why the Army's 2018 recruitment advertising was so flawed.

THOSE WHO SHOUT LOUDEST

It's no secret that the Army had been sinking money into recruitment with lesser results than ever before. Yes, the adverts were bigger and glossier, but the messages portrayed were flawed.

Their "Made in the Royal Navy" TV advert tells a story of someone becoming a bartender, and then suddenly finding purpose by joining the Royal Navy. The advert is almost emasculating in tone, making out the person was a loser (because of his career) until he joined.

The message is no longer "we need you", the message is "you need us"; and it's falling on deaf ears.

Their Twitter ads spoke directly to millennials, using name-calling as a tactic to engage with audiences.

The adverts mimicked the classic WWI poster in style, stating the army needs you, but then preferenced it by degrading the audience with an insult. "Phone Zombies", "Snowflakes", "Me Me Me Millennials"; it's rude in tone.

Yes, the adverts say the Army needs us, but they make sure to insult you beforehand. This is the advertising equivalent of spitting in a stranger's face, and then offering to buy them a drink.

THOSE WHO SHOUT LOUDEST

I honestly have no idea why they believed these adverts would work.

With both of the army and navy advertising campaigns, it appears their approach is to crush audiences before picking them up.

Does the Royal Navy only want people who have fallen on hard times, or should they be telling a different narrative that also targets more ambitious demographics?

And is it effective for the Army to be targeting people who (according to the stereotypes they are promoting) do not work well in teams?

Meanwhile the Royal Marines' recruitment adverts were everything the army and navy adverts couldn't be.

Instead of assuming who the audience are (which the Army and Royal Navy ads do), the Royal Marines show what they can become.

One advert focuses on a spider crawling its way up a marine who doesn't flinch, focused on remaining still and camouflaged whilst concentrating on their target.

Another simply shows the marines travelling down a dark, smokey river surrounded by debris and fire.

THOSE WHO SHOUT LOUDEST

The adverts are ominous in tone and don't generally show any actual "action", instead centering on the soldiers themselves and their unshakeable professionalism in the face of destruction and danger.

Most importantly, it's inclusive. "You can be more than you ever thought possible"; almost reminiscent of those iconic WWI posters.

Know when not to experiment with an idea.

What's better than a really good idea? Being able to recognise a bad one.

Even Amazon, arguably the biggest brand in the world, regularly makes mistakes detrimental to its worth. Well-intentioned ideas can unexpectedly devolve into monsters, ruining the original goal.

When Amazon made its marketplace more accessible for other businesses and individuals to advertise their own products, it should have opened up Amazon to new innovation and support for local businesses. To an extent it succeeded, as many businesses have been able to utilise Amazon, some even making it their main source of sales.

Unfortunately, the more open marketplace also invited less desirable sellers and businesses. Amazon has become infested with drop shippers, like ants swarming fallen fruit.

THOSE WHO SHOUT LOUDEST

Drop shipping, for those who are unaware, is when a person or company sells a product which they don't stock themselves. When they sell the product, it comes directly from the manufacturer or another supplier.

Drop shipping isn't an inherently evil idea. Many brands use drop shipping for their online sales, as it can be a great way to reduce running costs. For example, if you own a small clothing brand, you can use drop shipping to sell your clothes without needing to pay for warehouse space or staff. The manufacturing, packaging and shipping is sorted; so you can just focus on the marketing and designing apparel.

Technically this book is a product of drop shipping.

When people refer to "drop shipping", though, they don't tend to be talking about this general definition.

If someone talks about doing "drop shipping" or if you see it referred to in an article, it tends to be when someone is selling a generic product online (like a white coffee mug or a hamster wheel) and getting it shipped directly from the manufacturer in China to the consumer in the U.S. or the U.K.

THOSE WHO SHOUT LOUDEST

They're not creating a "brand" or looking to create repeat business, they're just trying to target impressionable consumers for easy sales.

The actual product the consumer buys is just some cheap knockoff item which would usually cost them a $1 if they bought it from AliExpress (which is what most drop shippers use for "buying" their goods), but because they bought it through the drop shipper it cost £20.

Amazon opening its doors to being a generic marketplace allowed drop shippers to add all sorts of crap, including items that imitate genuine brands.

For example, when buying ear protectors for my brother at Christmas, the best selling pair (and most expensive) were an off-brand pair re-boxed as a reputable brand.

As drop shipping continues to become a popular way for marketers to make a secondary income, it's inevitable that Amazon will become more saturated with this content. Within the next few years Amazon will potentially become another eBay, where genuine and bootleg are increasingly difficult to differentiate.

Nobody ever blames those selling the products either, they blame it on the website they bought them from (in this case Amazon).

Amazon's intention was pure, but by doing so they've potentially devalued their brand.

Understanding how to improve revenue without being tasteless is often a difficult subject, and one that seems to trouble a lot of internet based brands. Influencers often find themselves in hot water for which brands they promote or how they do it.

Even journalists struggle to strike a balance between generating revenue and reporting the news.

News websites are covered in advertising in order to maximise revenue per article, often to the point that it damages the usability of the website.

Reputable news websites often feature spammy adverts underneath their articles promoting mobile games and dodgy websites looking to collect your data.

Additionally, news websites are happy to advertise on pretty much any article they release, irrelevant on the topic. Even the video of George Floyd being murdered, every news website I saw had adverts on their articles or a paywall advertising their own paid subscription service. None of the articles I saw mentioned if they were giving any of this revenue to the family of the victim.

Media companies have to find a way of financially supporting news reporting, but the current system isn't working.

Articles are pushed out prematurely in order to improve rankings on Google and maximise reach on social media. The accuracy of the news is put second to the article's ability to generate clicks.

Of course this also expands beyond journalism. As mentioned earlier in this book, influencers often find themselves running into the trap of creating more shocking content for the sake of gaining views or a following.

In 2016, the app Vine (a social media and short-form video sharing platform) shut down. As a result, influencers who previously had made a living on Vine were forced to diversify into other social media platforms.

YouTube, in particular, saw many of the creators from Vine dominate the video sharing platform in 2017.

One of these creators, Logan Paul, was quickly growing on the platform.

THOSE WHO SHOUT LOUDEST

His hyperactive daily content was gaining a large amount of following, especially with younger audiences. Everyday there was a new video, and the content seemed to escalate in ridiculousness as time passed.

When talking about 2017 now, Logan Paul says that he gained an obsession with numbers. The views on each video, his followers and the amount of merchandise sold on his website; there was an internal pressure for the numbers to grow.

As a result, the videos became more over the top. Content began relying on shock value. Sexualising videos unnecessarily, breaking the law, and so on; whatever generates the most engagement.

As a result, Logan Paul's merchandise shop generated tens of millions of dollars in 2017, and it seemed as if nothing could stop the then 22 year old YouTuber.

Unfortunately, it only takes so long until this obsessive behaviour leads you to become detached from reality, which is what resulted in him creating a video documenting a suicide in the Aokigahara forest in Japan.

Whilst shock factor was initially paying the bills, the global coverage of this video resulted in Logan Paul's career becoming derailed.

From being one of YouTube's favourite content creators, to being distanced from the website in a matter of months.

That's not to say divisive content doesn't work from a commercial standpoint.

In 2019, a woman's razor company created an advert on Twitter that said the following:

> "Go out there and slay the day.
>
> *[brand name]* is committed to representing beautiful women of all shapes, sizes, and skin types because ALL types of beautiful skin deserve to be shown. We love *[model name]* because she lives out loud and loves her skin no matter how the "rules" say she should display it"

The advert featured a plus sized model at the beach in a bikini.

The advert is fine, reading more like a PR piece than advertising. However, it received thousands of responses and backlash.

Many criticised the advert for romanticising obesity, and many responded to those criticisms accusing them of fat shaming; this one advert somehow caused a huge argument across the social network.

It's worth noting that before this advert, the same company had posted other images with models of various body types and ethnicities (including the same model as in the beach advert). None of these photos had any backlash, and only got creepy responses from random men online saying they'd "hit that" and other perverted responses.

So why was this different?

The advert was clearly promoted to people who would respond aggressively (both positively and negatively). This then results in more exposure through people arguing over whether the image is or isn't "body positive". Because of this, all of the people responding's followers will also see the advert, and then they will potentially respond, too.

Additionally, the advert's text is perfect for getting responses. Whilst it looks positive, it promotes a non-existent ideology. I.e. There are no rules that say plus sized women can't wear bikinis, but the advert claims there to be.

They tried to do something similar with a transgender model within the prior months too, but received little response.

Unlike the beach advert, the transgender ad was promoted through platforms that support transgender rights. So, the response was positive, but it got a minuscule reach in comparison to the negativity the beach advert received.

Again, this is clearly because they promoted their beach advert to people who would react negatively, creating a divisive conversation that was designed to generate anger.

This approach to advertising is nauseating. At a surface level understanding of the ads they seem great, but underneath this thin layer of kindness lays a dark ulterior motive.

It's an advertising technique that has been used before, specifically by Russia during the 2016 U.S election. When it was used by Russia, the whole world freaked out, but when it's a popular razor brand their actions are accepted.

The result? Their stocks grew, proving that despite it being extremely unethical, it clearly worked.

If you're growing your brand, it's important to get outside opinions on a subject. Whilst controversy may help pay the bills, it can also destroy a brand. For the small short-term success that it can generate, is it worth risking everything else?

What can we expect from the future of brands and online marketing?

All industries are currently in an unpredictable phase. The Coronavirus (COVID-19) pandemic has resulted in many industries questioning their validity in 2020.

Office space companies are likely worried about workspace becoming abandoned as more individuals work from home, and many employees are likely worried that their job will be made redundant as companies begin to hire remotely in areas of the country that have cheaper housing (and therefore can be paid less).

So what will stand the test of time?

THOSE WHO SHOUT LOUDEST

As brands become more remote and more impersonal, I believe that better customer service and intimacy will have an increased value in the future.

This applies to every industry, in my opinion.

If you're a tradesman, this could mean being approachable and more tidy. If you run an online store this could mean offering live chat so you can talk to customers and help them find products that are right for them. If you have an OnlyFans profile, this could mean spending more time talking to clients.

Ultimately, better customer service means better customer retention, and people are generally much happier returning to spend money somewhere that makes them feel welcome, rather than where they feel ignored.

We already see this to be true with influencers. Those that do livestreams and interact with their audience can see huge amounts of money "donated" to them. An hour of livestreaming can surpass a month of advertising revenue from YouTube, for example.

Additionally, I imagine that people will be more interested in spending money with local brands as opposed to global online shops, mainly for similar reasons.

THOSE WHO SHOUT LOUDEST

As drop shipping pollutes marketplaces like Amazon and Ebay, people will become annoyed with the poor customer support and low quality of the imported goods.

As a result, I think there will be a resurgence of local brands able to profit from better quality and service.

If a brand is manufacturing a product themselves or using a manufacturer in the same country as them, they can also advertise the environmental benefits of purchasing through them.

Without having to import products from another continent, the brand avoids excessive shipping and can ensure that the product is made using ethically sourced materials.

The more local goods we buy, the less pollution is generated and the more we are supporting our own economy.

I believe people often forget that goods imported from abroad are often cheap because they come from countries where labour laws are more lax (meaning abysmal pay for workers or potentially child labour).

There's a big moral dilemma about supporting these companies, but I won't cover this as I'm not educated enough to paint the full picture. I will say, though, by supporting local brands consumers are able to be more confident in the working conditions of employees and the quality of the materials used.

That being said, I don't expect Amazon and Ebay to disappear, I just expect their demand to plateau and adjust. People will always want cheap products, and if they're looking for washing line pegs I doubt they'll attempt to find ones created by a local company.

I think the next big online marketplace will come from Honey, who are owned by PayPal.

So what is Honey?

Honey is the browser extension that saves your favourite influencers from bankruptcy.

I'm only joking, that's just a play on their famous ad spots' opening line, "Honey is the browser extension that saves you money".

Honey does what it promises; saving you money through discounts on online shops.

Honey makes money through an affiliate sales program. Essentially, if you make a purchase on a website and are using their browser extension, Honey will get an amount from the sale (if the retailer is part of Honey's affiliate sales program).

Part of how Honey provides discounts is through giving the user a percentage of their revenue from the sale. E.g. If Honey gets you a 10% discount on an online shop, they might have originally earned 25% from the overall sale, but split their revenue to create a 10% discount for you, leaving them with the other 15%.

Honey has been accused of making money through data collection at various points, with people suggesting that Honey will eventually sell your shopping patterns to advertisers in the future.

However, Honey denied the claim.

In my opinion, their next move is to create their own online marketplace to rival Amazon.

Honey could realistically be Amazon's biggest potential competitor if they choose to create their own online marketplace. With the cheapest prices on new products, purchases going directly to the retailer (meaning everything listed is authentic) and a more user friendly website design; Honey could potentially disrupt Amazon in a significant way.

THOSE WHO SHOUT LOUDEST

With thousands of retailers already working with Honey, it only seems like the natural progression of the company.

This would also explain why Honey continues to collect data from their users even though they're not selling data or using it to generate ads; they're potentially using it to determine their future marketplace's features and product ranges.

By monitoring how their users interact with other online shops and what products draw the most attention, Honey is able to create a blueprint for the most effective online shop possible.

When you consider that PayPal bought Honey for a whopping $4 billion, it seems unlikely that Honey will remain as just a browser extension.

Additionally, as the final bit of evidence for this claim, if you search for a product on Honey's website (after logging in), you'll notice they feature products on the website like an online shop. Instead of being able to buy the product directly from Honey, though, it just links to the product's page on the supplier's website.

Whilst just speculation, I'd be surprised if we didn't see Honey launch their marketplace within the next few years.

So, yes, whilst it seems as if everyone else in the industry believes that the near future will see artificial intelligence and robots dominate every industry possible, I expect to see almost the opposite.

Humans ultimately enjoy interacting with other humans. It's why lonely men choose to send women money on OnlyFans for 10 minutes of attention per day instead of paying to talk to a robot that simulates having a wife. Whilst a weird example, I think you probably understand what I'm saying.

Additionally, artificial intelligence (more commonly referred to as "AI") simply isn't as sophisticated as many people believe. At least, not the versions that the public has access to.

Google is very excited about their automated marketing tools in Google Ads. During my Google partner exam, around 70% of the answers Google wanted me to express were in favour of their automated campaigns.

But are the automated advertising campaigns all they are made out to be? Well, not really.

First thing you need to understand about AIs is that they don't understand intent. As humans, we can decipher connotations and which search terms are more likely to lead to a sale. Because of this, a human operated advertising campaign will tend to deliver a better quality of lead.

Whereas an AI run campaign will equally value people asking FAQs to an actual lead, or advertise for searches relating exclusively to your business (who would have got in touch regardless of the ad appearing).

Additionally, AIs will tend to prioritise quantity of quality. Meaning an AI will probably just focus on cheaper services/products that get the most searches, as opposed to more profitable ones that receive less searches per month; potentially not covering the cost of advertising.

You can't talk to the AI to explain these things. If you're finding the quality of leads or sales aren't what you expected, you can't talk to the AI about adjusting your marketing strategy. Instead you have two options; turn the advert off, or put up with the lacklustre results.

If a person is doing your campaign, you can talk with them and explore your options for adjusting the advertising strategy.

Realistically the best time to use an AI is when you don't have the time or knowledge to manage your own marketing campaign, but also don't have the budget to pay a marketing company to handle it for you.

Through machine learning the AI will try to deliver cost-effective leads or sales for your company, whilst you focus on doing the actual work.

As proud as Google is of their ability to provide effective automated marketing solutions, it still doesn't live up to the quality of human controlled advertising. As a solution for small business owners with a limited advertising budget, though, automated advertising could help take some stress away.

It's worth mentioning that the AI systems that companies like IBM and Google are creating for large companies are a different kind of beast, but these tools are unlikely to be available to small brands within the foreseeable future.

Small brands are ultimately the main employer of people within the UK, and by the time we see AIs infiltrate these markets I imagine we'll live in a very different world.

By that point I wouldn't be surprised if being an influencer was a more viable career for the average person, somewhat replacing the average sales role due to influencers being able to move products remotely and often more efficiently.

Even at the moment we're seeing the influencer industry quickly evolve and mould other industries along with it.

Following the lockdown during the current Coronavirus (COVID-19) pandemic, many businesses found themselves in a difficult position. In particular, the tourism industry, as people have postponed their holiday plans.

However, amongst all of this chaos, one industry has been booming; social media and content creation.

TikTok, unsurprisingly, kept creeping its way up the social media app hierarchy.

TikTok targets a younger demographic than its competitors, booming in popularity with "tweens" and young adults. Its content creators are also increasingly young, with some of the biggest stars being under 18 years old.

In many ways, TikTok is Vine 2.0.

Similarly to how all the major Vine stars moved into LA's Vine Street to collaborate and promote each other's brands, TikTok creators are beginning to form "content houses".

A "content house" is a property where a group of creators live (usually branding this group and the property with a name, such as "Hype House" or "Clubhouse") and where they are able to make their videos, with other content creators coming to the property to join in.

The more lavish the property, the better the perceived value of the group.

From LA mansions that look like they're from a renaissance painting, to penthouse suites; it's a big step-up from the bedroom in their parent's house.

It's definitely not an original idea – brand incubators have existed for a long time – but as with everything to do with social media, it's much faster and more temperamental.

One day the property is full of influencers getting millions of views, the next day the individuals within the house have all fallen out and are leaving due to drama; it's a highly dynamic and ever changing landscape. This is due to the age of these "content houses" occupiers, who are usually no older than early twenties.

For example, in the Hype House (which earlier this year was covered in The New York Times), the oldest influencer was just 21 years old, with many of the brand's stars being under the age of 18.

Young, impulsive teenagers with (as far they're concerned) a never-ending supply of cash are going to make frequent crazy decisions. Such as wanting a mansion, a Lamborghini, & to live with all of their rich friends.

The issue that influencers had, though, was that it's difficult to rent or buy somewhere when your income is so irregular. Sure, this month you made £10k, but a couple of months ago you were making £4.55 an hour at McDonalds.

Additionally, it tends to be difficult finding a letting agent who's comfortable with groups of people renting one house together (especially when most of them are under 18).

Airbnb fulfils this need. Sure, you're paying a premium for the property because it's through Airbnb, but you're able to fulfil your dream and quickly. You don't need to be locked into a year of living in the property together either, you can choose shorter renting periods which will better suit the influencers' spontaneous movements (or their career dwindling within their time staying in the property and having to move back home).

Influencers aren't the only young, successful group that are making a quick-buck and want to live a lavish lifestyle. Sex workers (including OnlyFans users), startups, and other "get rich quick" schemers are similarly looking for something to reflect their new found success.

Sure, it's a very temperamental way of living, but for many of these individuals their careers are short-lived or unpredictable.

Whether we like it or not, influencer culture is becoming a bigger part of everyone's lives. Social media apps like Instagram encourage people to seek validation from strangers; flaunting fat cat success whilst also having a picturesque social life.

So when young influencers begin renting houses with all of their friends, there tends to be a trickle down effect as their viewers also see it as a desirable life choice.

Sure, they can't afford a mansion in Beverly Hills, but they can just afford a family house in the nice bit of town. And, let's be honest, it seems a lot more impressive than living in their parent's house.

So whilst Airbnb is having issues due to the tourism industry being unpredictable, there's a good chance it could successfully pivot and market to young people as a solution to renting.

However, this is all just speculation, and could pan out to be as far off as cryptocurrency "experts" prediction that Bitcoin would reach $100,000 by the end of 2019.

THOSE WHO SHOUT LOUDEST

Marketing is an unpredictable industry, but that's often what makes it such an exciting industry to work within.

Online marketing's ability to interfere with politics is likely to become increasingly monitored by government bodies, and this will likely determine the future of the industry.

Whilst I want the industry to overall remain unchanged and to have no interference, there is the ongoing risk as political parties and activists utilise these tools more.

Also, as the availability of these tools become increasingly available, those looking to abuse them to exploit and scam also increase.

Luckily, following many controversies in the last several years, the companies and organisations that own these advertising platforms have begun putting safeguards in place to help prevent abuse.

From AIs being implemented that flag scammy adverts to ensuring that policies are in place preventing political parties from abusing advertising; whilst an imperfect solution we are seeing improvements to ensure these tools are not taken away from brands that need them.

THOSE WHO SHOUT LOUDEST

As advertising has become an increasingly big part of culture, it's highly unlikely that brands will ever completely lose these tools.

Even the journalists who criticise digital advertising are dependent on them for revenue.

Hopefully, we will see the world changed positively by those bold enough to utilise these tools, bringing about advances in technology and society quicker than before. This could be funding a product that helps the environment, or creating a technology that makes communicating with long-distance family members less difficult; advertising is what results in these products gaining the support to make them a permanent reality.

THOSE WHO SHOUT LOUDEST

Closing thoughts...

In the words of the fictional king of advertising, Don Draper:

"Change is neither bad nor good, it simply is."

Marketing is an ever changing industry, and one that is exciting to take part in. Despite all the negativity we constantly see in the media, I think it's a blessing that we live in a generation where this is all possible.

Hysteria will always surround new technologies regardless of what age you live in. No doubt that when electricity began to become widely adopted, someone probably claimed it was the devil's work. Or when flush toilets were introduced in homes, someone probably claimed that they prefer walking to their outhouse.

The current advances in technology that are occurring are changing the world for the better. The world is closer together than ever before, and I hope this continues to be the case.

It's amazing that during the pandemic (that is still happening at the time of writing) so many brands and services were able to stay open and operate efficiently. Of course, it hasn't and won't be all smooth sailing, but the damage that could have been caused has been largely reduced thanks to the technologies available.

It'll be interesting to see how different industries adapt and what new industries will emerge from the world changing in response to the pandemic.

Additionally, it will be interesting to know which industries see an increased interest due to the pandemic. For example, spy software is likely seeing an increase as companies want to keep an eye on employees.

The likelihood is that the majority of people will be reading this post-lockdown, but even then we won't truly know the long-term effects that the pandemic will have on many industries. This will become clearer in the following years.

Hopefully, for this book's sake, we see an increased interest in books.

I often use writing as a coping mechanism for stress and anxiety, and being able to positively channel that energy into a product (this book) is the most rewarding feeling in the world.

THOSE WHO SHOUT LOUDEST

20 years ago it would have been near impossible for me to publish a book, but thanks to the technologies available today, I'm able to independently publish my writing and share my thoughts with the world.

I'm not selling units like Fifty Shades of Gray, but it's exciting that hundreds of people have purchased or downloaded the books.

The last two books, to be honest, were a learning experience.

With each book released I aim to improve the reader's experience and the quality of the book that is produced. As my book is published independently through Amazon, the process of creating isn't ideal. I don't have an editor to make sure I haven't made any mistakes and I don't get an advance to pay for my time writing.

The books are ultimately a passion project, and I do them because I'm genuinely interested in what I'm writing about and want to share my knowledge with others.

My goal is for someone to read this book, find a topic in the subjects I've covered that they find interesting and go out of their way to research further, and then be inspired for them to create or innovate.

Overall, writing these books is a really positive and uplifting experience for me, and I'm blessed that people continue to support and appreciate my efforts.

If you've enjoyed the book and want to see more of my writing, head over to my website and subscribe (it's a free subscription). I release articles providing advice, talk about other companies, do Q and As, and recall my own experiences within different industries.

Thank you for your support and taking the time to read this book.

SirThorney.com